My Walk With Jesus Devotional Bible

31 Encouraging Devotions for Children Facing Cancer and Challenging Health Conditions

Jenna Sue Bennett

Kids of the King PRESS

Published 2015

Copyright ©2015 by Jenna Sue Bennett & Kids of the King Press

My Walk With Jesus Devotional Bible

Jenna Sue Bennett

ISBN—13 978-0-692-53274-4

ISBN—10 0692532749

All Scripture quotation, unless otherwise indicated, are taken from New International Version®, NIV®. Copyright © 1973, 1978, 1984 by Biblica, Inc.™ Used by permission of Zondervan. All rights reserved worldwide.

Scripture quotations marked NLT are taken from the Holy Bible, New Living Translation, copyright © 1996, 2004, 2007 by Tyndale House Foundation. Used by permission of Tyndale House Publishers, Inc., Carol Stream, Illinois 60188. All rights reserved.

Scripture quotations marked TLB are taken from The Living Bible copyright © 1971 by Tyndale House Foundation. Used by permission of Tyndale House Publishers Inc., Carol Stream, Illinois 60188. All rights reserved. The Living Bible, TLB, and the The Living Bible logo are registered trademarks of Tyndale House Publishers.

Scripture quotations marked ICB are taken from the International Children's Bible® *Copyright © 1986, 1988, 1999 by Thomas Nelson, Inc. Used by permission. All rights reserved.*

Scripture quotations marked ESV are taken from The Holy Bible, English Standard Version® (ESV®), copyright © 2001 by Crossway, a publishing ministry of Good News Publishers. Used by permission. All rights reserved."

Scripture quotations marked ISV are taken from the Holy Bible: International Standard Version®. Copyright © 2003 by The ISV Foundation. Used by permission of Davidson Press, Inc. ALL RIGHTS RESERVED INTERNATIONALLY.

Scripture quotations marked HCSB are taken from the Holman Christian Standard Bible®, Copyright © 1999, 2000, 2002, 2003, 2009 by Holman Bible Publishers. Used by permission. Holman Christian

Standard Bible®, Holman CSB®, and HCSB® are federally registered trademarks of Holman Bible Publishers. Unless otherwise noted, all Scripture quotations are taken from the Holman Christian Standard Bible®, Copyright © 1999, 2000, 2002, 2003, 2009 by Holman Bible Publishers. Used by permission.

Scripture quotations marked GW are taken from GOD'S WORD®, © 1995 God's Word to the Nations. Used by permission of Baker Publishing Group.

Edited by ChristianEditingServices.com

Photography Credits:

(Page 11 - "Boy/[WavebreakMediaMicro]/[Dollar Photo Club]")

(Guarded by God - "Boy/[inna_astakhova]/[Dollar Photo Club]")

(Pretty Inside and Out - "Girl/[Jessica Key]/[E+]/Getty Images" "Jesus/[Biblica Inc.]" "Beach/[Dollar Photo Club]")

(Pieces of His Plan - "Boy/[Blend Images - JGI/Jamie Grill]/[Brand X Pictures]/Getty Images")

(Hooray For Hats - "Boy/[Springoz]/[Dollar Photo Club]")

(He Picks Me - "Girl/[Dollar Photo Club]" "Rabbit/[Anatolii]/[Dollar Photo Club]")

(Thanks to Jesus - "Boy/[WavebreakMediaMicro]/[Dollar Photo Club]")

(Just Like Me - "Boy/[Jessica Key]/[E+]/Getty Images" "Jesus/[Biblica Inc.]" "Beach/[Dollar Photo Club]")

(A Box Full of Love - "Girl/[nanettegrebe]/[Dollar Photo Club]" "Gifts/[Africa Studio]/[Dollar Photo Club]" "Kitten/[Dollar Photo Club]" "Scissors/[Dollar Photo Club]" "Ribbons/[SM Web]/[Dollar Photo Club]")

(Running To Jesus - "Boy/[Yupiramos Group]/[Dollar Photo Club")

(My Mighty Angels - "Boy/[Dollar Photo Club]")

(Jesus Cries Too - "Girl/[Tom Merton]/[OJO Images]/Getty Images" "Jesus/[Biblica Inc.]")

(A Hero Named Joseph - "Boy/[lemonadelucy]/[E+]/Getty Images")

(Precious Promises - "Boy/[Paul Bradbury]/[OJO Images]/Getty Images" "Jesus/[Biblica Inc.]")

(Puffy Paintings - "Girl/[Dollar Photo Club]")

(Bubblegum Blessings - "Boy&Animals/[zmijak]/[Dollar Photo Club]" "Wall/[kav777]/[Dollar Photo Club]")

(A Smile from Jesus - "Boy&Iguana/[Fuse]/Getty Images")

(Calling Jesus - "Girl/[Thanasis Zovoilis]/[Moment]/Getty Images" "Jesus/[Biblica Inc.]" "Hand/[Emma Kim]/[Cultura]/Getty Images")

(Super Me, Super You - "Boy/[BlueOrange Studio]/[Dollar Photo Club]" "Dog/[iko]/[Dollar Photo Club]")

(I Found You - "Girl/[Samuel Borges]/[Dollar Photo Club]" "Balloons/[Africa Studio]/[Dollar Photo Club]" "Ducklings/[Africa Studio]/[Dollar Photo Club]" "Gift/[karandaev]/[Dollar Photo Club]" "Chick/[Anatolii]/Dollar Photo Club]" "Eggs/[marog-pixcells]/[Dollar Photo Club")

(Talking to Him - "Girl/[gekaskr]/[Dollar Photo Club]" "Jesus/[Biblica Inc.]")

(Little Special Me - "Boy/[Jenna Sue Bennett]/[Private Photo]" "Beach/[Dollar Photo Club]" "Dinosaur/[Jenna Sue Bennett]/[Private Photo]")

(My Bestest Friend Forever - "Jesus&Girl/[Biblica Inc]")

(Helping Hearts - "Boy/[Dollar Photo Club]")

(My Brother Jesus- "Boy/[Dollar Photo Club]" "Wall/[stocksolutions]/[Dollar Photo Club" "Jesus/[Biblica Inc.]")

(My Heavenly Daddy - "Girl/[Kinson C Photography]/[Moment]/Getty Images")

(Creator Of The Universe - "Boy/[Dollar Photo Club")

(A Heavenly Home - "Girl/[slp_london]/[Dollar Photo Club]" "Duckling/[Anatolii]/Dollar Photo Club]")

(Baaaaaaa! - "Boy/[Tatjana Kaufmann]/[Moment Open]/Getty Images" "Barn/[Peter Kim]/[Dollar Photo Club]" "Field/[Fyle]/[Dollar Photo Club]" "Lamb/[DLILLC/Fuse]/Getty Images" "Jesus/[Biblica Inc.]")

(Angels Around Me - "Girl&Cat/[Dollar Photo Club]")

(Look There's Jesus - "Boy/[Kohei Hara]/[Digital Vision]/Getty Images" "Sky/[Matthew Bowden]/[Dollar Photo Club]" "Jesus/[Biblica Inc.]")

(A Letter From Jesus - "Jesus"/[Biblica Inc.])

(Page 75- "Boy/[nanettegrebe]/[Dollar Photo Club]" "Sky/[RFsole]/[Dollar Photo Club]")

Photos marked with the credit "[Biblica Inc.]" are used by permission. Please see below…

Kimberly and her children— Lathan, Lannah, & Lauren

Dedicated in loving memory of...

Kimberly Irene Wiles-Suitt

1969—2010

I love you, Aunt Kimmie. Love, ~Jenna Sue

My Walk With Jesus Devotional Bible would not exist, if not for my Aunt Kimmie...

She inspired my heart—

Her battle with stage four lung cancer was the first time I had ever seen the effects of cancer. It was so hard to see her having to go through those extremely challenging times physically and emotionally. My heart went out to all of the families dealing with cancer, especially those with children who were facing cancer. I remember how she always read out of a children's devotional book to her kids every night. This gave her special close time with her children, and brought priceless memories to cherish forever. Together, through that little book, they all found encouragement and strength to help them through the hard times. It was then that I decided to write a devotional book of encouragement for children facing cancer.

She encouraged my dream—

Many lives were encouraged by her great strength and loving spirit as she fought her cancer. I am one of those many. I'll always remember how it didn't matter how weak she was physically— her love remained solidly strong. She was always there for everyone, giving of herself in every way she had. She encouraged me to write My Walk With Jesus Devotional Bible, to share the love of Jesus with precious children, and their parents. She was so thankful that her life inspired a tool to bring hope and strength to families with children facing cancer.

Her faith shined beautifully—

She trusted her Father in Heaven daily for the strength and love she needed to walk with Jesus. I'll always remember the day she shared with me her favorite Bible verse.

"But those who trust in the LORD will find new strength. They will soar high on wings like eagles. They will run and not grow weary. They will walk and not faint." — Isaiah 40:31 NLT

On earth, Aunt Kimmie walked with Jesus. Now, in Heaven, still she walks with Him. But now... She holds His hand.

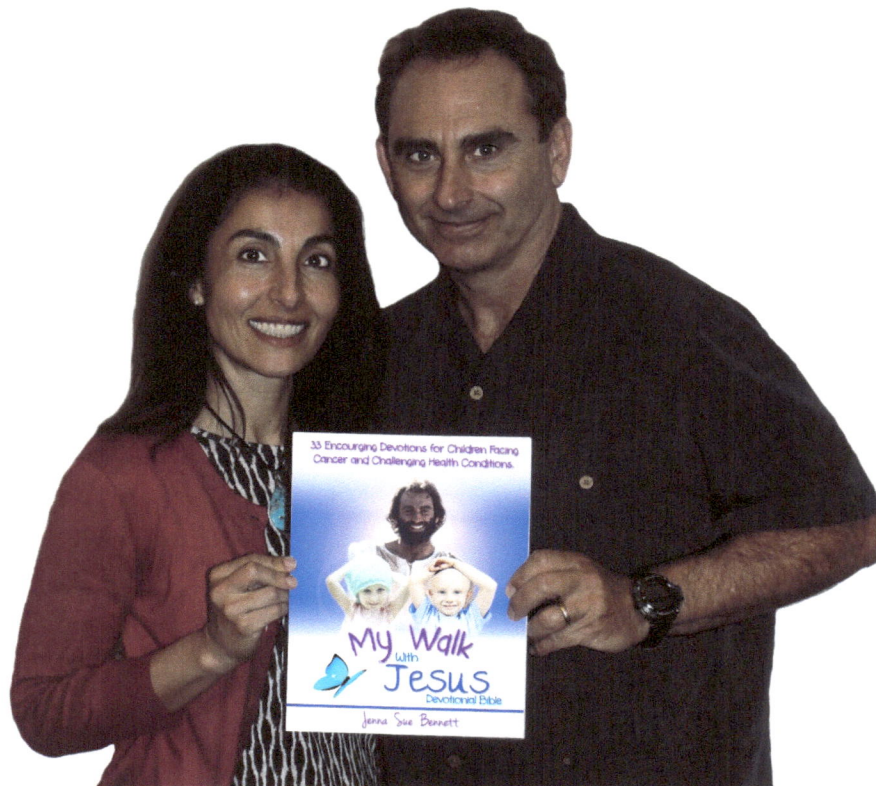

Bruce Marchiano & his wife, Maria

"Jenna Sue Bennett is a wonderful young lady with her eyes solidly on the Lord, and serving people in His name. Her written words will surely bring healing and touch hearts, as they reach with the love of Jesus. Thank you, Jenna, for your wonderful book."

Bruce Marchiano

Actor, Best Selling Author, Producer, and Founder of Marchiano Ministries

Bruce's portrayal of Jesus in the 1993 movie *The Gospel According to Matthew* inspired Jenna to use the pictures from that movie in My Walk With Jesus Devotional Bible.

Sharon Puterbaugh & Jenna Sue Bennett

"Jenna Sue Bennett is a talented young lady. Her talent and love for Jesus are very evident in this book. This book is going to be a blessing to many people! It is a pleasure to know Jenna."

Sharon Puterbaugh

Administrative Assistant for Marchiano Ministries

"From the first time I read My Walk with Jesus Devotional Bible, I knew it was very special. I can't stop talking about it to my family and friends. The concept of writing a devotional book for sick children is straight from the Father's heart. I can't wait to see the doors the Lord opens for Jenna Sue Bennett and her inspirational book. The best is yet to come."

Dixie Phillips

Award Winning Children's Author, Dove Award Winning Songwriter, & Editor of My Walk With Jesus Devotional Bible

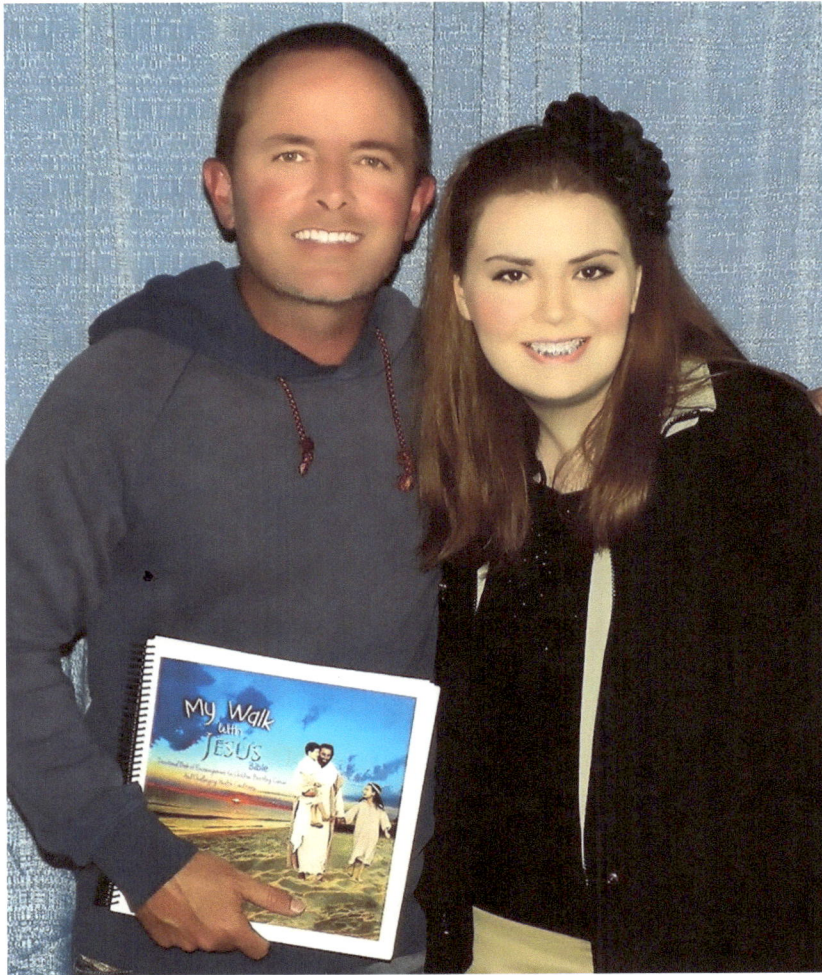

Chris Tomlin & Jenna Sue Bennett

Chris Tomlin holding the very first printed copy of My Walk With Jesus Devotional Bible, with the original cover design.

August - 2014

Chris Tomlin

Dove & Grammy Award Winning Christian Singer & Songwriter

Table of Contents

Guarded By God

I will not be afraid, for you are close beside me, guarding, guiding all the way. – Psalm 23:4 TLB

Hey there! I'm Cody and I have a pet elephant named Squash. I named him that because he's super ginormous and he squashes lots of stuff! We have lots of silly fun together. We stomp our feet all around and make the **WHOLE** world shake! But we have to be careful because Squash has some holes in his big tummy, and his stuffing is starting to fall out. Don't worry though, Grandma's gonna sew him up.

Squash is almost always brave and strong, but right now he's biting his toenails. He's never been sewn up before, and he's a little bit worried about what all is going to happen. I know how Squash feels because sometimes I get scared too. When I first got cancer, I was kind of afraid of big hospital machines. When I visit the hospital, sometimes Dr. Donald orders tests to see pictures of what's going on inside me. He uses a giant machine that has super x-ray vision. The first time I went inside the machine I was really scared. I didn't want to go in there all by myself. I grabbed Daddy's leg and looked up at him, "Why can't you come with me, Daddy?" Then he got down on his knees and put my cheeks in his hands, "Cody, I'm your daddy, and I want to come with you and take care of you so much. But I'll be here for you when you come out. And you won't be alone, not for one second. God is **ALWAYS** with you. He'll be holding you in that big machine." I wanted to trust, but I didn't know how to. "Daddy, I can't see God. How do I know he'll be with me?" Daddy put his nose up to mine, "Because He's your father, just like I am. You trust me, when I say I'll be here for you when you come out. Don't you?" I nodded. "You can trust Him with your whole heart. When He makes a promise in His word, The Bible, He keeps it." Then Daddy hugged me tight, and I went inside. The machine went "bang" and "buzzz". But even with all that noise, I heard a little something in my heart. I think it was a special whisper from God, telling me how He was right there with me, protecting me. I felt like He was my Daddy from Heaven, holding me tight.

Now when I go to the hospital, I say "I will not be afraid! You are right here guarding me, God." Even when I go places where no one else can go with me, not even my elephant Squash, God is right there. I'm really glad I have a big, strong God to guard and shield me wherever I am. God will always take care of you too. He loves **YOU** just like you are the **ONLY** child He has! And even though we can't see Him, He's right here holding us. We don't have to be afraid of anything! I'm so glad we have our mighty God protecting us. Look, even Squash is brave now that He knows God will take care of him!

Today's Talk to Jesus

Dear Jesus,

When I do things that make me kind of scared, I know You're right there with me. And I know You're here now, right by my side, guarding me with Your powerful love. I couldn't be in more perfect arms. The things I'm afraid of might seem huge to me, but Your love is bigger than **EVERYTHING**! Thank You for Your super strong love that keeps me safe wherever I go. I sure do love You.

In Your precious name, Jesus. ~ Love, Me

Pretty Inside And Out

Don't be concerned about the outward beauty of fancy hairstyles, expensive jewelry, or beautiful clothes. You should clothe yourselves instead with the beauty that comes from within, the unfading beauty of a gentle and quiet spirit, which is so precious to God. – 1 Peter 3:3-4 NLT

Hi! My name is Katie. What's your name? I **LOVE** to look pretty. I bet you do too. I love to dress up in my favorite pink pajamas and paint my nails a gorgeous purple, but I've been kind of sad lately. It all started when I found out I had cancer. My doctor ordered medicine that helps me get better, but it made my hair start falling out too. I didn't know why every time I combed my hair, bunches of it came out in my hairbrush. I tried to put it back on my head, and it just fell off again. I even tried to tape my hair back on, but it just wouldn't stay there. My mom told me that my medicine would make it fall out, and how it would grow back soon.

One morning before school, I looked in the mirror and saw that all my hair was gone. I just started crying and ran to my mommy. She hugged me really tight with one of her special squeezes. I told her, "I just want my hair back, so I can look pretty again." Mommy kissed one of my tears, "Katie, you don't need hair to make you look pretty. You have the most beautiful big, blue eyes, and a precious smile." Then she put her finger on my nose. "And the cutest little nose I've ever seen. You are a beautiful princess... you're the daughter of the King of kings. He made you **PEREFCT**– inside and out." Then she told me something else that really made me feel pretty again. She said, "The Bible tells us that real beauty doesn't come from the outside... not from hair, jewelry, or clothes. True beauty comes from inside your sweet little heart!"

What Mommy told me really helped me think. Some kids worry that their friends won't like them if they don't have fancy clothes, expensive perfume, or long wavy hair. But those things don't really matter at all. True beauty comes from inside my heart, not my red lips and cheeks or pretty hairstyles. When I love other people and have God's super perfect love in my heart, it makes my heart look just like His. That's the **MOST** awesome way to be beautiful! That kind of pretty is **SOOO** precious to God, our Daddy in Heaven. He loves it when we shine with His perfect overwhelming love. We are His precious little children. He thinks we are perfectly beautiful... and **HE** knows because He made us!

Today's Talk to Jesus

Dear Jesus,

I know I'm truly beautiful when my heart shines with your love. If I look in my mirror and feel sad because I don't look exactly like I used to, help me to know that I'm perfectly beautiful to you. You made me with your perfect love, and you love me more than I could ever understand, exactly the way I am. I'll always be your pretty little princess.

In Your precious name, Jesus. ~ Love, Me

Pieces of His Plan

"For I know the plans I have for you," says the Lord. "They are plans for good and not for disaster, to give you a future and a hope." – Jeremiah 29:11 NLT

Hi there! I'm Theodore, but Mom calls me "Teddy Bear". You can call me that too if you want. Do you have something you just love doing more than anything else? I do. I love to put jigsaw puzzles together! Mom and Dad bought me an extra awesome teddy bear puzzle for my birthday. I was so excited because it had 200 pieces! I worked for days putting each piece in its perfect spot. It took a really long time because it had **TONS** of tiny pieces— a half-of-an-ear here and a fuzzy little bellybutton over there. I thought it would never all come together to make a picture of a teddy bear... but it sure did!

I found out something really cool one day when Mom and I were putting my puzzle together. We couldn't find one of the pieces, so I bent over and looked under the sofa. That made me start coughing and I couldn't breathe very well. Mom helped me take some medicine and it made me feel better. "Mom, why do I have to be so sick?" She wrapped her arms around me, and gave me the biggest hug in the whole world. She said, "The hard things in life we have to go through are kind of like these puzzle pieces. We can only see a little tiny piece of our life at a time, but our Heavenly Father sees **ALL** of it, all put together. We don't always understand what is going on, or why we have to go through these things that are so hard for us. But we can always trust that God will take care of us, and help us through everything, **ALWAYS**." Then she got her Bible from the bookcase and showed me a special little part of God's puzzle plan. It said that God has a special plan for my life, a good plan to give me hope and a future. I know that He puts each piece of my life into its perfect place to make me— His perfect little masterpiece that He treasures with all of His heart.

I'm so thankful God loves us so much! We don't have to worry, no matter what we're going through, because we know He has a very special plan to take good care of us and to give us His love always. And the best thing of all is this— He will never leave us all by ourselves, even when our world feels like it breaks into a zillion little puzzle pieces. He just wants us to give Him all the little pieces of our broken hearts, and He will put them all back together with His love. And He will never stop loving us with his perfect, precious love— love so **BIG** we could never even understand it.

Today's Talk to Jesus

Dear Jesus,

Thank You for taking care of me every day of my whole life. Sometimes I don't understand why it seems like my life falls apart into itty bitty pieces, but I know one day You will show me all the times You put my life back together again. You never want me to go through sad or hard things, but I know that You hold me and help me through them. I trust You with every little piece of my life! I am **SO** precious to you. I love being Your little **MASTERPIECE!**

In Your precious name, Jesus. ~ Love, Me

Hooray for Hats

Fix your thoughts what is true and good and right. Think about all you can praise God for and be glad about. – Philippians 4:8 TLB

Howdy! How are y'all doin' today? It's mighty nice to meet ya, Partner. I'm Buckaroo! Well, that's not my real name, but that's what my Daddy calls me. I'm a rootin' tootin' cowboy! Some days I'm even Sheriff Buckaroo at Dodge City. Other days I'm a cowhand at the O.K. Corral. I know how to lasso chairs… I mean cows. My hospital room… I mean my ranch… is full of livestock. I've always got loads of work to do, rescuing the animals that have gotten themselves in a pickle.

I've got my own ten-gallon cowboy hat. Would you like me to tell you all about it? Well, not too long ago, my doctor said I have something called cancer. I had to take some very strong medicine to make the bad cancer cells go away. And the medicine made my hair start falling out. I think I still have a few left up there, but not very many. Mommy told me I needed a special hat to keep my head warm. She went to town and bought me one, but I didn't like wearing that hat at all. I thought it made me look silly. I got upset, started crying, and yanked it off my head. It just didn't feel like my hair did. I didn't understand why I couldn't just have my hair back.

Mommy scooped me up in her arms, and I sat on her lap while she read me a verse in the Bible. It said to think about good and happy things, and to find things we could be glad about in our life. She said we were supposed to behave humbly and not grumbly. I told Mommy I was sorry. She squeezed all the grumpy out, and all I had left was a big smile.

Mommy said, "Buck, I think you could have lots of fun wearing special hats. You could pretend to be anything you want to be in a hat. How about if I take you to that special costume store and let you pick out the most awesome hat there!" So we hopped in the pick-up truck, and we were there in no time.

I just couldn't stay still because I was so excited when we walked into that store. I had a hard time deciding which hat I wanted. I could be a firefighter, a chef, or even a doctor! But **THEN**… Mommy and I saw the ten-gallon cowboy hat. We knew right then and there it was the one for me! Now I go around lassoing all the wild horses on the prairie… I mean hospital. I can't say I don't miss my hair, because I do, but I just love my cowboy hat. I'm really happy Jesus helped me find just the right one. I'm His little buddy.

Today's Talk to Jesus

Dear Jesus,

Thank You for the special little things You give me every day. Help me to always think about the good things You give me because they're all around me. Sometimes even the things I think are going to be rotten, turn out to be a lot of fun! And I have a lot to be glad about because we're partners, and I'm your little rascal.

In Your precious name, Jesus. ~ Love, Me

He Picks Me

If God cares so wonderfully for the flowers that are here today and gone tomorrow, won't He more surely care for you? – Matthew 6:30 TLB

Hey, where did you come from? I guess you were hiding behind that giant sunflower over there. You sneaked up on me! Would you like to help me water Grammie's flowers? Thanks, it's a **BIG** job. My name is Princess. Well, that's what my daddy calls me. I love being his little princess. But I'm also a princess that likes to get muddy! So mostly, I wear my overalls instead of a princess dress. I just love helping Mommy and Grammie in our beautiful flower garden. We plant roses, buttercups, dandelions, tulips, marigolds, and lilies. But do you know what flower I love most of all? Sunflowers! I think they are the prettiest flower in the whole entire universe! They're so huge and colorful! And the little birds love to land on them to eat the yummy seeds. I like them too, **YUMMY** in my tummy.

I learn about all kinds of cool things while we're busy in the garden. One time, Grammie asked me, "What do you think is more special to God, you or the flowers?" I thought about that, "Hmm, flowers are so pretty. So He must spend a lot of time making them that way. Is it the flowers?" I asked. Grammie smiled, "Well, there is a time in the Bible where Jesus was telling us about that. He said, 'God cares so wonderfully for all the flowers, even though they only last a few days before they go away. But He cares **SO** much more than that about you!" I thought that was the most super incredible cool thing I had ever heard! The Creator of the **UNIVERSE**, thinks we are His most precious creation!

I used to work in our garden almost every day. But when I got cancer, the doctor said I needed to rest a lot more. I can only go outside and help water the pretty flowers once in a while. I have to stay inside most of the time. I sure miss all the beautiful flowers and little animals when I have to be in my room. It gets pretty boring in there sometimes. Whenever Grammie comes to see me, she brings me sunflowers from her garden. She says, "When you look at them, you can remember that special verse I told you about in the garden, the one that tells about how God takes care of the flowers. I want you to always remember that you, little Princess, are so very precious to God, your Daddy in Heaven. So you can always trust Him to take good care of you, especially when you're sick. You are His favorite little flower, and if He could pick any flower in His **WHOLE** garden, He would pick you first!" That really made me giggle!

I am in the very best arms ever and I'm so thankful He takes the most amazing care of me. I sure can learn a lot from my flowers. They never have to worry about anything and I don't have to either. After all, I am a princess! I'm the King of king's little daughter, His flower girl, and He loves me a whole bunch!

Today's Talk to Jesus

Dear Jesus,

Please help me to always remember that You're taking care of me always... every second, of every minute, of every day. Thank You for teaching me with Your beautiful flowers just how super special I am to You. Help me not to worry about anything because You promise to always take care of me, even more than the beautiful flowers. I love that you pick me first. I'll be your little flower forever.

In Your precious name, Jesus. ~ Love, Me

Thanks To Jesus

Give thanks in everything, for this is God's will for you in Christ Jesus. – 1 Thessalonians 5:18 HCSB

Howdy! I'm Jayden. Let's have a talk, Partner! How's about if I tell you about my big-ol' teddy bear, Chuckles. I think you'll like this story. Ok, here goes.

Well, when I got sick with cancer and had to stay in the hospital, I missed my home. And I was kind of scared too. I grabbed Mama's ears and pulled her close to me, "I just want to go home, right now. I want to go see puddles!" He was my brand new puppy I got for my birthday. We couldn't bring him to the hospital, because he makes a lot of puddles on the floor. Mama saw that my tears were creeping out. So she climbed up beside me on my hospital bed, put her arms around me, and squeezed me real tight. She put her nose right up to mine, "Jay, I think we need to talk to Jesus about how we feel afraid." I let go of Mama's ears, closed my eyes and laid my head on her shoulder. First, we started telling Jesus how scared we were, but then we thanked Him for all the ways He's been helping us get through the hard times, and for **ALWAYS** being here for us, no matter what. When we got through talking to Jesus, we both felt a lot better. It was like Jesus pulled a special smile out of His pocket, just my size… and it fit **ME** just perfect!

"Mama, remember when I first got sick? I was afraid of needles, and Jesus helped me to be brave whenever the nurses had to give me my shots, or test my blood." We both wiped each other's tears all away. "I sure do, my little Jay, and I am **SO** proud of you. See, Jesus has been helping us and carrying us through this **WHOLE** time. He'll keep helping us to be brave and strong, I just know He will!" Later that day, Mama got me a special present from the hospital gift shop. Can you guess what it was? Yep, it was Chuckles, my big-ol' teddy bear.

I pulled him out of that big bag, and man you should have seen the smile on my face! Mama said "Now, every time you look at your bear you can remember how Jesus helps you to smile. And no matter what bad, sad, crazy, mixed up things happen, you always have something you can be thankful for. The biggest thing is that His love never, **EVER** goes away, it just keeps getting bigger, and Bigger, and **BIGGER!**" I thought about how Jesus sends us special things to remind us how big His love is for us… like my Mama, who always takes care of me and gives me her love. I wrapped my hand around her finger, "I love you, Mama." She smiled, and gave me a big bear squeeze. "I love you too, Partner." Then she giggled and said, "Jesus even sends things for us to chuckle about." She rolled me over and tickled my tummy… then my giggles **SUPER** spilled out! Then she tucked my fluffy Chuckles under the blanket with me. He reminds me that I always have things to smile about… and they're all from Jesus. "Mama, I think I'm gonna name him Chuckles." Mama winked, "I think that's a perfect name." Now **YOU** know why I named my teddy bear Chuckles. I'm so thankful Jesus giggles with us too!

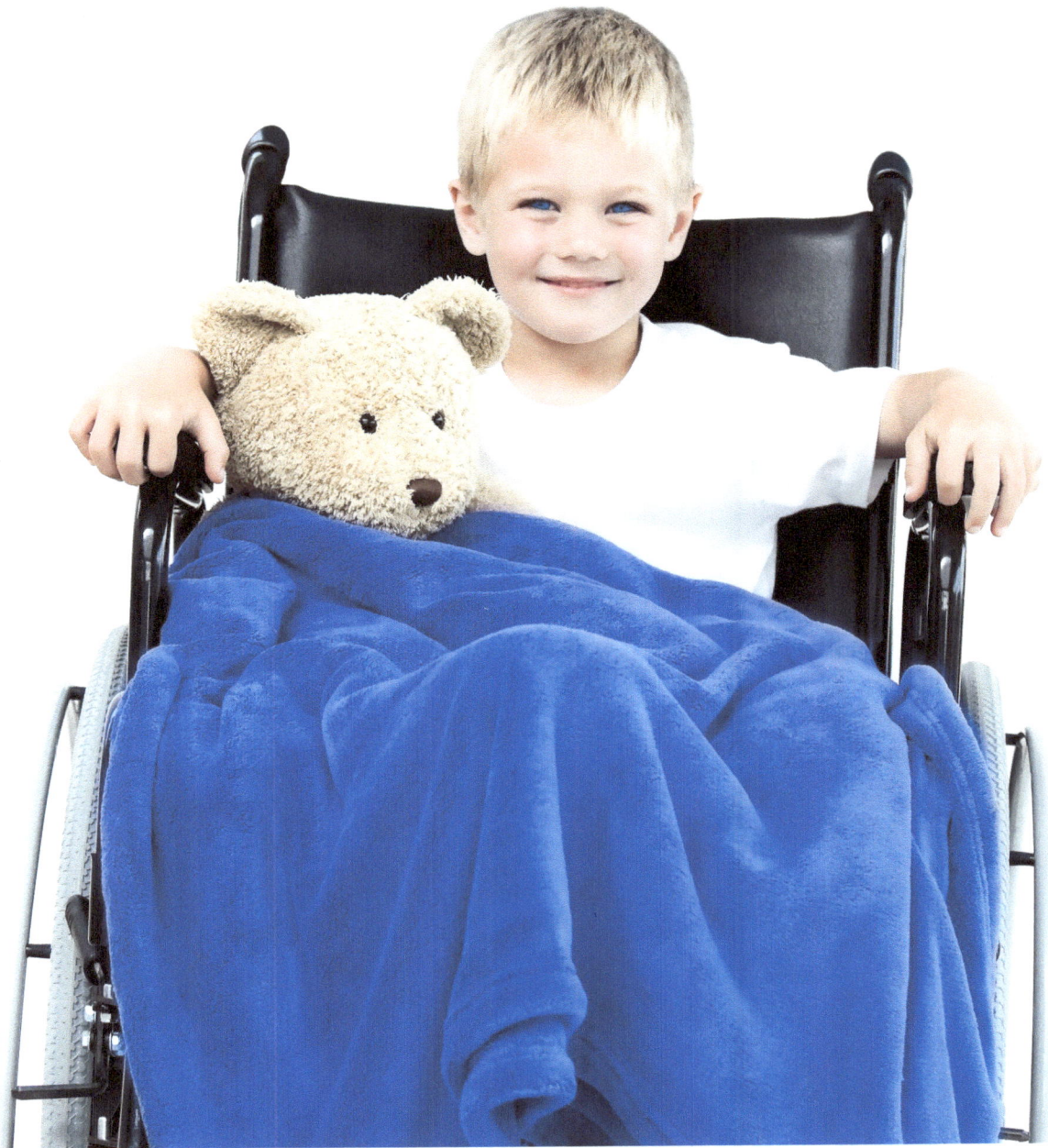

Today's Talk to Jesus

Dear Jesus,

Thank You for every little way you show me that you love me. You show me every day that you take care of me no matter what. You even send me things that surprise me… and things that make all my giggles come out. Thank You from the bottom, **ALL** the way to the top of my heart.

In Your precious name, Jesus. ~ Love, Me

Just Like Me

But Jesus said, "Let the children come to me. Don't stop them! For the Kingdom of Heaven belongs to those who are like these children." – Matthew 19:14 NLT

Hello! My name is Joshua. And I'm special! I know because Jesus told me that! I'm so glad He loves me and is always telling me how special I really am. You might wonder how Jesus talks to me. Well, one day our pastor said if we want to hear Jesus talk to us, we have to read the letter He gave us– it's called the Bible. After Church, I told my pastor I really, **REALLY** wanted to hear Jesus talk to me. So he gave me a little letter from Jesus, just my size! Now, wherever I go, I tuck my little Bible in my pocket. And when I need to know what Jesus wants to tell me, I've got all the answers right here with me!

A few days ago, I was playing with my friends. I couldn't do all the things they did, or play some of the games they played. I tried running fast, but I got dizzy. Some of the kids told me that I'm different because I have cancer. I have to stop and rest a lot more. And sometimes they say I look funny because I don't have any hair. The medicine I take that makes my cancer go away, made it fall out. Some of the kids don't understand how I feel. They said, "Joshua, you can't keep up with us." And that made me sad, and I even got kind of mad too. I went off by myself and found a big tree to sit under.

I tried to not think about the mean things they said to me. But I wanted to know what Jesus thought about me. Did He think I was different too? I took out my Bible– I mean– my letter from Jesus. Maybe there was something that He said in there about me. I prayed that He would tell me just what He thought about me. Then I closed my eyes, opened it up, and guess what I found? I found the most amazing story **EVER**. It was all about kids just like me. They went to go see Jesus. But, Jesus's friends were trying to make all the little children go away. All the kids wanted to do was spend time with Jesus, but the friends thought Jesus was too busy to see them. And then Jesus came up to the children. He told his friends, "Don't you stop them! I want them to come to Me! Heaven belongs to people who are just like them. They're so very special to Me!" And then I found another cool time in the Bible, when Jesus's friends asked Him who would be the most important person in Heaven. Guess what He did? He called a little boy, just about like me, to come sit on His lap. He said, "Whoever is humble, just like this little child, will be the greatest person in Heaven."

Isn't that just so cool? If Jesus took up for all the kids, and kept telling his friends how special they are, then we must really be **SO** special to Him! Wow! If He loves us that much, and loves spending time with us, we don't need to worry what anyone else in the whole wide world thinks about us! I hope you have a little Bible you can read. Time with Jesus will make you feel super awesome too. I just know it!

Today's Talk to Jesus

Dear Jesus,

Thank You for loving me a whole lot! I'm not really sure why I'm so special to You, but it sure makes me feel great to know I am! I love to close my eyes and pretend I am one of the children you held on Your lap. You're even holding me on Your lap right now! It doesn't matter if other kids make fun, I'll go have fun with You! You love me **EXACTLY** the way I am! And you made me to be **JUST LIKE ME!**

In Your precious name, Jesus. ~ Love, Me

A Box Full of Love

Three things will last forever— faith, hope, and love— and the greatest of these is love. — 1 Corinthians 13:13 NLT

Hi, my name is Charity. I love my name! I love it because it means love, and I love a lot of people, especially my parents. They love me a whole bunch too. When I got cancer, they worried about me a lot. I have to live at the hospital for a while, so I can get the right medicine. My doctors and nurses keep a close eye on me. My mom and dad take turns spending the night with me at the hospital. Sometimes they get sad and their hearts hurt for me. They're always here doing so much to show me how much they love me.

The other day I was thinking up a way I could do something special for my parents. I wanted to show them just how much I love them, and that I'm so thankful for all they do for me. I was stuck in my hospital room, so I couldn't go to a store to buy a present for them. I thought and thought but I didn't know what to give them. So I asked Jesus to please help me think of something **SUPER** special to put big smiles on their faces. I opened my Bible and read the verse about how the greatest thing of all is love. **POP!** Jesus gave me a **REALLY** great idea! When my nurse came to check on me, I told her about my plan. Well, she thought it was just perfect, so she hurried to get me some supplies. She brought me an empty box, pretty paper, colorful ribbons, tape, scissors, and bunches of big beautiful bows. Then I measured, and taped and wrapped until it was all just perfectly perfect. I set it on the foot of my bed for my parents to be **SURPRISED** when they came back.

I was **SO** excited! I just couldn't wait for Mom and Dad to open the special present I made just for them. When they got back, I reached out and handed them their gift with both hands and a **BIG** smile. They carefully opened the box. They peeked inside… and it looked like it was empty. But I told them that it wasn't empty at all! It was jam-packed **FULL** of **HUGS** and **KISSES** just for them. Mom smiled the biggest smile I've ever seen! Daddy squeezed me so tight with tears coming down his cheeks. I think it was the best present I ever gave them! I want to give them more of my love every day. I hope I can be there for them like they're always here for me. Thank You, Jesus, for giving my family Your special love that runs over and spills out. The more love we give away, the more we have! Jesus will give you and your family the love you need too. He never runs out of His love. It's more contagious than the chicken pox! If we have **LOVE**, we have **EVERYTHING**.

Today's Talk to Jesus

Dear Jesus,

Thank You for my parents and all the super special love they give me. Their love and hugs always make my heart smile. I want to give them big smiles too, and take all of the hurts right out of their hearts. I don't always know what they need, but You do. Please show me how to give them the best present of all – **MY LOVE!** Please let Your love shine through me, right to their hearts. When I wrap up all my love and send it to You, You send me **SO** much more to give away!

In Your precious name, Jesus. ~ Love, Me

Running to Jesus

Come to me, all of you who are weary and loaded down with burdens, and I will give you rest. – Matthew 11:28 ISV

I'm so glad you came to see me today. My name is Matthew, but my nickname is Rascal. That's what everyone calls me all the time, so you can too. I guess that name lets you know what I'm like a little bit. Daddy says before I got sick I was "stuck on go!" My super favorite thing to do was to run fast. Mommy said if I had been a racehorse, I would have won first place in the Kentucky Derby. Grandma told me she had raised her four little boys but never saw one as fast as me. **NOBODY** could catch me! But then I got sick and everything changed. Doc says I have a heart problem that not many kids have, and it makes me really tired. If I get up and run around too much, my heart starts to hurt and I get super dizzy and weak.

One day, I was outside playing baseball with Daddy. I tried to run across the yard, but I just couldn't do it. I fell down in the grass. Daddy saw me trying to make my tears stay in my eyes. He picked me up and put me in his favorite comfy camouflage chair, and wiped the dirt off my pants. I just let all my tears start running out and told him, "Daddy, I can't run like I used to. What's wrong with me?" Daddy got on his knees on the ground in front of me, and put his hands on my heart. He said, "Rascal, Jesus wants you to run for Him in a different kind of race…" I didn't mean to, but I interrupted him. "Daddy, I just can't run in a race for Jesus. I can't win– my heart won't work right. I don't want to run a race for Jesus and not win." Daddy wiped my tears away and told me, "You have a precious heart just like Jesus. That's why He wants you to run in this race for Him. It's not the kind of race you can lose either. Jesus wants you to run to Him when you're tired and have lots of hard things going on in your life. He will help you rest. You can run to Jesus, even sitting in your chair! His arms are wide open for you, **ALWAYS!**"

I tried what Daddy said and it worked. Every time I ran to Jesus, He helped me. When I don't feel good and can't get out of my bed, I run to Jesus and He holds me tight in His arms. So, if you are sick and don't feel good, like me, **RUN!** Run as fast as you can to Jesus's arms. You can do that when you talk to Him and read about Him in the Bible. The best news of all is that when we run to Jesus, He runs to us. Will you race me to Jesus? Catch me if you can. Ready! Set! Go!!!

Today's Talk to Jesus

Dear Jesus,

I'm so glad I can always run to You no matter what I am going through. Thank You for caring so much about me that when I'm weak and I don't have the strength to get up, You run to me. And right where I am, You pick me up and carry me. I'm so glad You hold me in Your precious arms. I'm so glad You gave me a super special heart, just like Yours. I have a **BIG** heart, and I love **YOU** with the **WHOLE** thing!

In Your precious name, Jesus. ~ Love, Me

My Mighty Angels

For he will order his angels to protect you wherever you go.
– Psalm 91:11 NLT

Hi there! Cameron is my name, and I love airplanes and helicopters! Really, I love everything about flying through the ginormous big blue sky. Sometimes I even dream I can fly. That is so fun! One day I found out I was going to my new hospital, a place where they help kids with cancer get better. And guess what... I got to ride there it a **REAL** helicopter! A lot of people got me all set up, and I had to have my medicine while I rode. I had lots of funny tubes and equipment from the hospital, all in that tiny helicopter! I just couldn't wait till they finished getting everything ready so we could **TAKE OFF!**

Finally... **ZOOM** we went– up, Up, **UP** and **AWAY!!!** I couldn't believe how teeny–tiny everything on the ground looked when I was way high up in the sky. It was so awesome! I could see for miles. I saw a whole bunch of funny geese, and I wished I could reach out the window and catch them! I could have even grabbed the fluffy white clouds. They looked just like cotton candy, and I bet they taste like it too. Yum! All the houses on the ground looked like dollhouses, and the cars looked just like my toy race cars.

Sometimes when I fly, I feel really close to God. I don't know why because Mommy told me God is everywhere. It doesn't matter where we go... God is always with us. I guess seeing the beautiful blue sky and the huge puffy clouds made me think about how **AMAZING** and **GREAT** God is. Some of the clouds even looked like angel wings. And just when I was about to get just a little bit scared, I saw those big angel clouds and they made me think of my Dad's favorite Bible verse – Psalm 91:11. God says He will tell His angels to protect me wherever I go. Isn't that **SO** cool? Even in the sky, God is holding me and His big strong angels are right beside me! I don't have to be afraid of anything... God is protecting me wherever I'm going and whatever I'm doing!

If you ever have to do something that makes you nervous, like flying in a helicopter or going to a new place, you don't have to be afraid at all. But, if you do get scared... remember how God has His mighty angels all around you, guarding and protecting you. God always protects us with His **POWERFUL** love.

Today's Talk to Jesus

Dear Jesus,

Thank You for Your perfect promises to me. I'm so glad You always send Your angels to keep me safe. I know that I don't have to be afraid at all… Your **AMAZING** love and protection is **WAY** stronger than anything I could ever be afraid of. And Your love for me is even **WAY** bigger than Your mighty sky! Wow!

In Your precious name, Jesus. ~ Love, Me

Jesus Cries Too

Jesus Cried. – John 11:35 GW

Hi, I'm Rebecca. Come sit with me a little while, so we can talk. I have cancer, and I have to live in the hospital. It's really hard for me sometimes. Sometimes I get scared, and hurt. Sometimes I cry. A few nights ago I couldn't sleep, so Mommy held me close in her sweet arms and sang to me. The song she was singing was about Jesus, and how He loves us.

I was listening to what the song said, and I asked her, "Mommy, I don't understand. If Jesus loves me, why does he let me hurt?" She brushed back my hair. "Becca, Jesus does love you, with all of His heart. And He would never want you to hurt. You are so very precious to Him. He feels every pain with you, and cries every tear with you. He loves you, and He will help us get through this." I still didn't understand. "But Mommy, Jesus is perfect. He doesn't cry." My tears were spilling down my face as Mommy kissed my nose. "He *is* perfect, and He loves us with a *perfect* love. That's why He *does* cry, because He loves us SO much." She put her hand on my cheek and wiped away all my tears. She got her Bible, and read to me two little words, 'Jesus cried.' "See Precious… in the story, Jesus went to see His friends. And His friends were sad, because their brother died. They were crying. Jesus loved His friends, just like He loves you. He cried with them, and His heart hurt with them." I couldn't believe it, I thought somebody as important as Jesus *never* cried. Mommy told me more, "I know with all my heart that Jesus is always holding you when the cancer makes you hurt. He feels our pain and understands our hurts. When we're sad, it makes Him even more sad. Rebecca, when you hurt, I believe with all my heart that He hurts with you. And when I can't be here to hold you, He is *always* holding you."

Mommy held me close and squeezed me tight. I looked up at her and tears were running down her cheeks too. I wiped them all away, and gave her kisses. She smiled her prettiest smile."Becca, just like Jesus knows exactly how our hearts are broken, and hurting– He knows exactly how to put our hearts back together with His PERFECT love! He wants to put a big, special smile on your face." I asked Mommy another question, "Mommy, why does Jesus love me so much?" She smiled again. "Because you are so very precious to Him. Jesus loves you so much, He died for you on the cross. He did it so we will be able to live with Him in Heaven forever and ever! His heart hurts when we hurt, and He cries when we cry. He is the best Friend we will ever, ever have. He always knows how we feel and He always takes care of our hearts. He will never, ever leave our side. And even when we're hurting together with Jesus, we can share smiles together with Him in our hearts, because He loves us so much more than we could EVER understand."

I hope what my mommy said helped your heart as much as it helped mine. Jesus sure does love you. I know with all my heart… He loves you with OVERWHELMING love.

Today's Talk to Jesus

Dear Jesus,

You have the sweetest heart. Thank You for loving me so much that You hurt for me on the cross. I love that you always hold me when I hurt and cry. You're just so perfect. You cry when I cry, and You smile when I smile. Even when we are hurting together, we can share smiles together in our hearts. My heart is Yours, Jesus.

In Your precious name, Jesus. ~ Love, Me

A Hero Named Joseph

Nothing above us, nothing below us, or anything else in the whole world will ever be able to separate us from the love of God that is in Christ Jesus, our Lord. – Romans 8:39 ICB

Hi there. This here is my pet turtle. His name is Toby, and I'm Little Joe. He's Toe and I'm Joe! My mom and dad named me after a cool guy in the Bible named Joseph. I love to read all about him. Hey, would you like me to tell you his story? He was not your average Joe, you know… He went through a bunch of hard times, and a lot of things happened to him that he just couldn't understand. But no matter how tough his problems were, he always tried really hard to trust God. Joseph's own brothers were mean to him, and he was even thrown into prison for no reason at all. Even through all of that, he knew in his heart that God was **ALWAYS** with him, even when it seemed like he was all by himself. He tried his best to remember that God loved him more than he could ever understand, and that God was helping him– no matter what happened.

My story is kind of like Joseph's. A few months ago, I got really sick. My doctor said I have cancer. For a while, I couldn't go to school or play outside with my friends. I had to stay in my bed a lot. That made me sad, and even though Mom and Dad tried to always be with me, I felt alone a lot. Sometimes when I have my treatments I start to feel lonely, like Joseph felt when he was in prison all by himself. But then I talk to God in my heart. I know He always listens, and every word I say is super special to Him. That's one of the cool things about God. He hears me even when other people can't. He's so amazing and He always loves me, no matter what I do or where I go! If I climb to the top of the **TALLEST** tree, His love is with me. And if I hop in a submarine and zoom to the bottom of the **DEEPEST** ocean, His love is with me. So even when I feel alone, I just need to know that I'm really with my all powerful God, my Father in Heaven, who loves me more than I could ever even try to understand. **NOTHING** will ever be able to take His awesome love away from me.

Joseph tried to remember that God always loved him, no matter how tough things were for him. He really got stronger when he trusted God through the hardest times. Our Father had a special purpose for Joseph. He became a great leader and saved the lives of many people. It took a while– like my Toby turtle here… I've been waiting forever for him just to cross this page! But Joseph was glad he trusted his Father's love. Our Father is our Daddy in Heaven, and He will love us forever! He said in His Word that **NOTHING** could ever keep us away from His love. I'm so glad I'm **HIS** kid!

Today's Talk to Jesus

Dear Jesus,

I love You with all my heart. Thank You for never leaving me when I go through tough times! Help me to be like Joseph and always trust You no matter how big my problems are. Your love is awesome! I'm glad it never gives up or runs out on me! Nothing can **EVER** take Your incredible love away from me. I am Yours forever.

In Your precious name, Jesus. ~ Love, Me

devotion 13

Precious Promises

The LORD always keeps His promises; He is gracious in all He does.
— Psalm 145:13 NLT

I'm Isaac and I love to hideout with S'mores. I bet you're thinkin' I love to sneak around and eat those sticky campfire cookies. You know, the graham crackers, marshmallows, and chocolate all smooshed together. Well, I do think s'mores are the **YUMMIEST** thing in the entire world, but this time I'm not talking about yummy stuff. S'mores is my teddy bear! He has been an awesome buddy to me, especially since I got cancer. He makes me feel awesome when I've been feeling true blue. S'mores and I love to race each other on my airplane simulator game— I win most of the time! Some days I feel too sick to get up, so Mom and Dad let me play some video games while I'm still in my bed. S'mores is right there with me. Some days I feel too sick to play a game or watch a movie. When that happens, my little buddy and I crawl under the covers together, and pretend we're camping. S'mores always understands when I don't feel good. The medicine I take makes my sickness get better, but sometimes it sure makes me feel really crummy. I get frustrated sometimes when I don't feel like doing the things I want to do.

A few days ago, I didn't feel like doing anything at all. Mom and Dad came in my room and they brought the big, blue Bible with them. Dad said… "We're going to learn about some of God's promises from the Bible together." Mom read a super cool verse about how Jesus always keeps His promises. Then we talked about one of those promises and what it means. Dad said, "Isaac, Jesus promises to never, ever leave you alone— not even for a single second! He will always hold you through the tough times. And when He makes a promise, it is never, **EVER** broken."

I've been thinking a whole lot about what Dad said, and I know he's right, but sometimes I wonder if Jesus is *really* with me. I know I can't see Him, but sometimes I like to imagine fun and silly things Jesus would do with me. He would play doctor with me and take care of my teddy, S'mores. We would eat campfire S'mores together too. Yum! You know, I bet He really does all those cool things with me. We can have all kinds of crazy fun time together because His love is so **BIG**!

This time that I've been sick has helped me learn a lot about God. I've found out that He loves me more than I could ever even understand. When I talk to Him, He helps me to trust Him about everything, even if I still don't understand it at all. When I don't feel good, I think about Him being with me, and that helps me to be strong. He is always spending special time with us, and watching us— just as if He only had one child to love. That is **SO** incredible to me… **ALL** of His love, **ALL** of the time. I'm so glad that when my Father in Heaven makes a promise, He always keeps it.

36

Today's Talk to Jesus

Dear Jesus,

Thank You for always keeping Your amazing promises. Please help me to have really strong faith in You and every promise that You've promised me. I know You're right here with me, and you love spending time with me. You help me with everything I go through, and You love me more than I could ever even try to understand. I love You too, Lord. And I want to make You a promise from my heart. I will always live for You and love You forever... and I promise to keep my promise too.

In Your precious name, Jesus. ~ Love, Me

Puffy Paintings

Your strength shall be renewed day by day like morning dew.
– Psalm 110:3 TLB

Hi there. I bet you're wondering what my name is. I don't think you could ever guess the right name. I'll give you a hint. My first name starts with an A. Ready? Nope, my name isn't Amy, Amanda, or Alexa. Give up? My name is Apple Dumpling! Well, that's what Mommy and Daddy call me! They gave me that nickname when I went to Grammy's house and gobbled up all of her super scrumptious apple dumplings. My real name is Autumn Dawn, but I like Apple Dumpling better.

I like to play outside with my friends. Since I started treatments for my cancer, I'm not strong enough to play freeze tag, monkey in the middle, or hide and seek, but I enjoy just being with my friends. While they play all kinds of running and jumping games, I **LOVE** to look up and watch amazing clouds go by. I can see a whole **ZOO** in the sky! There are lions, giraffes, and monkeys! Ooh-ooh-ah-ah! Look, there's a ginormous elephant and a spotty giraffe! **WOW**! Sometimes I even see pretty princess castles with strong brave knights. Did you know if you look really hard in the clouds, you can see just about anything?

Every time I watch the clouds, I remember how much God loves me. He paints **GIANT** pictures in the sky just for **ME**! God loves me so much, and He loves to have lots of fun with me. He gives me special things to do when I'm too tired to run around and play. I get tired a lot faster than my friends, and I can't play as long as they can, but God is my very best Friend. He gives me my strength every day. I can always count on Him to help me do whatever I need to do. He knows when I'm weak and tired. When that happens He always gives me special, fun things I can do with Him.

I love how He takes such good care of me. I am forever His little Apple Dumpling. He promised to love me always– now on the earth, and forever when I get to Heaven with Him. He will always be my Heavenly Daddy who gives me His strength every day! He overwhelms me with His perfect love. Who wouldn't want to be His little child? He showed us how much He loves us when He gave us all He had– His Son Jesus! I'm so glad we're His little children. Aren't you?

Today's Talk to Jesus

Dear Jesus,

Thank You for painting special pictures in the sky just for me! I just love looking at them, especially on the days I don't feel good. Thank you for giving me my strength every day. I'm so happy I can look up in the sky and see Your special paintings. The fluffy clouds always make me think about how **BIG** your love is for me. You love to have fun and play with me. We use our imaginations together, and we always will. Your love for me is even bigger than all the puffy clouds in the **WHOLE** sky. My love for **YOU** is too.

In Your precious name, Jesus. ~ Love, Me

Bubblegum Blessings

God will supply all your needs from his glorious riches. – Philippians 4:19 NLT

Hi there! I'm Tyler and this is my cat, **BuBBleS**, and my dog, **PoP.** I think bubblegum is the greatest invention in the entire universe. Don't you? Doesn't everyone? Do you know why I love bubblegum so much? Well, sometimes when I go to the doctor, Mommy says I'm a little squiggly wiggly worm! I get all nervous and my tummy does flip-flops. I just can't sit still at all. Sometimes I even feel like crying, but Mommy came up with a plan. She promises to give me a whole pack of bubblegum if I sit really still when I visit the doctor, and while I have my breathing treatments. Whenever I'm being a rascal, she always shows me my pack of bubblegum and nods her head. I know that means I'm supposed to sit very still and do what the nurse and doctor tell me to. When they're all finished, I get my bubblegum. I think it's a pretty good plan. It always takes my wiggles **FAR** away.

My very favorite flavor of bubblegum is cotton candy. It's the absolute best ever, I promise! To me, everything is great when I have my cotton candy bubblegum. But a few days ago, there was a big problem. Before I went to my doctor's office, Mommy and I went to the store to pick up a pack of bubblegum. And do you know what? They were all out of my cotton candy bubble gum! I was so sad and mad. I stomped all around the store. I just couldn't believe it! Just when I felt like crying, Mommy picked me up and squeezed all the sad out of me. She said, "It's ok, Tyler. God always gives us all the things we need. He even cares about the smallest, tiniest things we want too. He wants us to talk to Him about everything." I grinned just enough to show my missing teeth. Mommy always knows exactly what to say to help me feel all better.

Mommy and I prayed and asked Jesus to help us find some yummy bubblegum. And do you know what happened? You'll never, ever guess! My Grammie came to my doctor's office and guess what she had in her bag– three whole packs of cotton candy bubblegum! Mommy and I looked at each other and grinned. We knew Jesus had answered our little prayer. He knows everything we need and cares about each little thing– even about a little pack of bubblegum! I guess I learned one thing through my bubblegum adventure– if God cares enough about me to give me a pack of my favorite bubblegum, I know He cares so much more about the sickness I'm going through. He will always help us through the tough times. He wants us to trust Him about everything. He loves us more than we could even understand. I hope my little bubblegum story will help you to know how much God loves you too.

Today's Talk to Jesus

Dear Jesus,

Thank You so much for giving me all the things I need and even sending me some special little things just because You love me. I know You don't have to do that, but I'm so thankful You do. Thank You for loving me more than I can even imagine. I love You too, Jesus!

In Your precious name, Jesus. ~ Love, Me

A Smile From Jesus

Do Not Worry. – Matthew 6:25 NIV

Hey there! I'm Adam! And this little green guy is Spike, my Iguana. He's pretty good at making me smile. But I want to tell you about the bestest buddy I've ever had– His name is Jesus. I can talk to Him about anything! He always hears me, and He always answers me. I can't hear Him with my ears, but I know He's always talking to my heart. And even when I'm sad or worried, He can give me a smile.

My mom told me about a time in the Bible when Jesus was talking to some people on a mountain. He told them a lot of amazing things about our Father in Heaven. He said that our Father puts the petals on every flower, and feeds every little bird! He also told them not to worry because our Father loves **US** so much more. And He's **ALWAYS** protecting us and taking care of us, no matter how tough things get.

Sometimes it's hard not to worry about all the problems we have. I know when I got cancer, I was scared and I worried if I would ever get better. Then when I had to take lots of medicine and have my treatments, I started to worry a whole bunch more. So I found a little quiet place at my favorite tree and I sat down and looked up at the puffy white clouds. I just told Jesus I wanted Him to hold me and help me. Right then and there, He calmed my little heart– just like He calmed the stormy seas. Jesus doesn't want me to worry about anything. My life is in His strong hands, and my life is so, so precious to Him. I'm riding in His arms! I know He's carrying me through all these hard times, and He's carrying you too!

Whenever you start to worry, just remember what I've told you. Jesus wants to be your bestest buddy too, and He doesn't want you to be sad or worried. He comforts us and sends us smiles with so many special things… a hug from Grandma, a ride on Daddy's shoulders, colorful books, and even iguanas that like to rub noses! He will help you to have a smile that could only come from trusting Him with all your heart. We can trust Him because He loves us so much that He gave up everything He had. He died for us, so we could live with Him forever. His love for us is **SO BIG**. I'm really glad to have a smile that comes right from Jesus.

Today's Talk to Jesus

Dear Jesus,

Thank You for being my very best buddy! You're always right here for me, holding me on your lap. I'm glad You love me more than I could ever even understand. Thank you for taking my worries away. Even when I forget and start to get scared…You calm my heart. And when the smile on my face just won't work, You fill up my heart with Your love, till there's no more room for worry. Thank You for giving me my smile. And I know You're smiling with me. You make my heart smile too big to fit in me!

In Your Precious Name, Jesus. ~ Love, Me

Calling Jesus

The Lord is close to all who call on Him. – Psalm 145:18 NLT

What a beautiful day to have a brand new friend! Hello, I'm Lily. I have a best friend named Emma. We love to talk on the phone together about all kinds of crazy, amazing things. She tells me about Mr. Wigglesworth, her **GIANT** goldfish. He goes *bubble-bubble* and gobbles up all the food he can find. I tell her about the cute things my baby brother does. We laughed and giggled forever when I told her how he learned to blow bubbles while Mommy feeds him carrots. There were messy carrots all over our kitchen for weeks! Mommy would rub and scrub the walls, but then the next day she would find more orange spots. It was a mess! Emma giggled and said she always feels happy when she talks to me. I guess that's why we're best buds.

A few months ago, I got test results that said I have cancer. I had to go stay at a hospital that was a long way away from my house. Emma's Mommy said she could still visit with me on the phone sometimes so I wouldn't feel too lonely. I told her about my treatments and what my hospital room was like. And I talked to her about the huge machines that make really loud sounds, like when my house was being hammered together. But I was glad that I got to wear earphones and listen to soft music. It helped me not to hear the loud noises so much. I also told her that I don't like a lot of people coming in my room all the time. But even though I don't know them, they're always nice to me. Emma always listens, but she doesn't really understand the things I talk about. She's never been in a hospital. Whenever we get on the phone, pretty soon we always have to hang up because my doctor or nurses come in again. When that happens I feel really lonely and sad, but then I think about what my Grandpa Georgie taught me. He said, "Jesus is your **PERFECT** best Friend, and you can talk to Him **ANY** place and **ANY** time."

I told Mommy what I remembered from Grandpa Georgie and she said, "Lily, let's talk to Jesus a little while." I liked that idea a bunch. "Ok, Mommy! But, don't we have to use fancy words when we talk to Jesus, cause' He's really important. He's like the most important guy ever!" Mommy giggled. "No, some people think they can only talk to Him about special things, and use big, fancy words. But Jesus likes for us to talk to Him right from our hearts. You can talk to Him about absolutely **ANYTHING**! The Bible says He's close to us when we talk to Him." I gave Mommy a really big squeeze and a super big smile. "Really, Mommy? I could think of all kinds of things to talk to Him about!" Mommy said, "I know with all my heart that He listens very closely to every word you say to Him, and every word you say is **SO** precious to Him." Then Mommy and I talked to Jesus and sent Him a **BIG** hug too.

When I call Emma from the hospital, I can hear her with my ears, but she's still really far away. Jesus is always right here with me, and I can talk to Him **ANYTIME** and **ANYWHERE**! I'm so glad we can tell Jesus about everything– the wonderful surprises, the super fun times, and even the hard things that make us feel scared or lonely. He always hears everything we say and we don't even need a cell phone! Really!!!

Today's Talk to Jesus

Dear Jesus,

Thank You for always listening to me when I talk to You! Thank You for loving me more than I could ever understand. I'm so glad You always stay right here beside me and understand how I feel when I'm scared or feel lonely. Thank You for holding me in Your precious arms. I love You with all my heart!

In Your precious name, Jesus. ~ Love, Me

Super Me - Super You

Wait patiently for the LORD. Be brave and courageous. Yes, wait patiently for the LORD. – Psalm 27:14 NLT

Ahoy, mate! This is Captain Caleb Courageous checking in from my Imagination Station. Right here beside me is my super dog, Sergeant Peanut Butter. He likes sandwiches. We love to put on our super-gear and fly through the big blue sky! You should see my super-duper shiny sword. It's the biggest sword on the planet! It has powers that are outta this world. Do you want to know what my sword really is? Well, I'll tell you all about it. My sword is the Bible, and it has the power to change your life forever. It helps you when you're stuck in a big old mess! That's what it did for me.

About a year ago, I got test results that said I have cancer. I was feeling really confused, so I went to visit Nana and Papaw for a while. We sat on the porch swing and talked about a few cool things in the Bible. At first I didn't really understand, but then all of a sudden Nana read this part, "Be brave and courageous!" Right then, I scooted up tall in the swing, and I knew that Bible verse was just for me. "I **AM** brave, Nana. And when I gave Jesus my heart, he filled it **ALL** the way up with courage! He changed me from an ordinary little seven-year-old boy to Captain Caleb Courageous!"

Did you know Jesus wants **YOU** to be a superhero too? Well, He does. And we get the best end of the deal. We trade our fear for courage and our worries for strong faith! Now that's some kind of trade, don't you think?

The best way to become a superhero is to be buddies with Jesus and read His Word. The Bible gives us strength we never even knew we had. My mom and dad said Jesus has sure carried them through this hard time while I've been sick. My mom knows that our Father in Heaven is listening to all the prayers everyone has been praying for me. Daddy told her that there is amazing power in prayer! He knows God loves it when we talk to Him, and He answers our prayers in special ways. But one thing that takes **SUPER** strength is waiting on Him. When we spend time waiting on Him, it makes us even stronger. Only God can give us that amazing strength. God is the most awesome superhero **EVER**, and He uses His powerful love to help us through the tough times.

I'll let you in on a little secret– even though I have this cape, I can't really fly. But when Jesus comes to take us all home, I'll fly all the way to Heaven with Him. And while I'm waiting on Him, I can be brave and courageous. Let's go read God's superhero manual together. Then you can trade your fears for courage too. Shooom!

Today's Talk to Jesus

Dear Jesus,

Thank You for Your amazing Word that gives me courage when I'm afraid. I want to be strong, brave, and courageous just like You were when You were here on the earth. You're my most favorite Superhero of all times! I can't wait until we all fly home with You.

In Your precious name, Jesus. ~ Love, Me

I Found You!

When you search for me with all your heart, you will find me.
– Jeremiah 29:13 ICB

Hi, my name is Kayla. And these are my little friends— Quackles, Waddles, and Mr. Peep. I love to play games. Do you? My favorite game is hide and seek. I love pretending I'm a detective and finding clues hidden all around me. Grandma and Grandpa came to see me at the hospital, and brought me a **GIANT** magnifying glass so I could see better for my secret mysteries.

One day Mommy took me on an Easter egg hunt at our church. It was **SO** fun! All of us kids were full of giggles as we searched for the eggs. We looked and looked for a really long time, but not one of us found a single egg. Most of the kids just gave up. I was really tired but I just couldn't give up. I had to find those eggs! So mommy pushed me around in my wheelchair for a while. She's a lot of fun!

I remembered how good Jesus was at finding lost things. I told my best friend, "Chelsey, Daddy told me that one time Jesus found him when he was lost. Let's ask Him to help us." So we said a prayer and asked Jesus to help us find the eggs. We decided we would look together. Then I got out my detective magnifying glass and guess what? Yep, you guessed it. Jesus answered our prayer. We found all the eggs! They were hidden together in a **GIGANTIC** pile! I wish you could have seen them all. They were decorated so pretty. Some were painted really bright colors all over. Other ones had polka-dots, stripes, zigzags, and there were even some with butterflies!

Chelsey and I were so excited, we jumped up and down. We were thanking Jesus for helping us find them, and just then we spotted one huge egg at the tippy-top of them all. We opened it up and discovered a yummy chocolate heart with a special Bible verse wrapped around it. I read it out loud to Chelsey. "When you search for Me with all your heart, you will find Me!" We knew it wasn't talking about the eggs. It was talking about Jesus! We knew if we searched for Jesus by reading the Bible and talking to Him, we would find Him! We were **SO** excited to find all the Easter eggs! And even more excited to find one filled with treasures about Jesus! Finding Him is sweeter than **ALL** the candy in the candy store!

Today's Talk to Jesus

Dear Jesus,

I love You soooo much! Thank You for teaching me I can always find You when I look for you. You're the greatest Treasure of all, and I don't even need my magnifying glass to find You. Thank You for loving me and giving me the best and biggest hugs in the whole world. I will always search for You with all my heart, and I **SURE** do love to find you.

In Your precious name, Jesus. ~ Love, Me

Talking to Him
Never stop praying. – 1 Thessalonians 5:17 NLT

Nice to meet ya! My name is Gracie and I love making new besties. Well, really all my friends are my besties. But I especially enjoy having girl chats on my tablet with my very best friend, Isabella. We talk for hours and hours, and we never, **EVER** want to stop. We talk about absolutely everything– from apple flavored lip gloss, to zebras getting loose at the zoo! You name it… we've talked it! Yup, **EVERYTHING**!

Lately, I haven't been able to talk to her very much because I've been pretty sick. The doctor said I have cystic fibrosis, and it is getting worse. It makes me have trouble talking and even breathing. Sometimes it feels almost like I'm a little tiny fish out of my water. Mommy tells me I need to turn off my tablet, take my medicine, and rest. That helps me feel better, but I really miss getting to talk to Isabella. She misses me a lot too.

One day I was crying and my daddy came in my room. He asked me what was wrong, and I told him how I much I missed talking to my friend. Daddy said, "Gracie, you have a best Friend who never leaves you alone, not even for **ONE** second. He wants with all His heart to talk to you and give you His precious love, **EVERY** minute, of **EVERY** day, **ALL** of your life! Do you know who I'm talking about, Pumpkin?" I wiped away the tears from my eyes and said, "Yes. You're talking about Jesus. Right?" Daddy nodded. "You can always talk to Him, whether you're having a fun day, or even if you're coughing and feel like you can't breathe. His precious Word, the Bible, tells us to 'never stop praying.'" Then he scooped me up in his arms and squeezed all my sad out. "If you think this is a big squeeze, Pumpkin, you just wait 'till you get a hug from Jesus one day!" We giggled together.

Now I talk to Jesus **ALL** the time! I don't even need to bring my tablet with me. I chat with Him at the doctor's office, the mall, my school– even when I am having my breathing treatments and I can't talk out loud, I can still talk to Him in my heart. I probably talk his ears off! But, He's always right here to listen, and he goes through every single second with me, the good ones and the bad ones. My heart even talks to Him while I'm asleep! I wonder what I say in my sleep. Hmmm??? Anyway, I tell Him about anything and everything, all the time. He loves to hear me talking to Him from my heart. And His heart is always, **ALWAYS** talking to me too!

Today's Talk to Jesus

Dear Jesus,

Thank You for always being right here with me and listening to every word I say to You. I don't know how I would ever make it through the tough times without You to talk to. I just love being Your bestie, Jesus. Having a heart-to-heart chat with You makes me not think so much about the hard things in my life, and helps me see all the perfect blessings You send to me every single day. I don't even have to say amen, or bye, or anything like that, because our special chats never, **EVER** have to end! Thank You for being so perfect! I love You!

In Your precious name, Jesus. ~ Love, Me

Little Special Me

You gave me life and showed me kindness. And in your care you watched over my life. – Job 10:12 ICB

Hi there! Oh, don't worry about me. I know it's very unusual, but Mr. Pickles only eats vegetables. That's why he's so green! He has severe food allergies, just like me. Only I'm not green, I'm Noah. I'm an animal research scientist! I **LOVE** every single critter created! Mommy says that God blessed me with a special loving heart, and lots of joy. I love to talk to everyone I see. I'm glad I can share my joy with you! I think being happy is the best way to make new friends, and I love making friends... of **ALL KINDS**!

Friends can come in all shapes and sizes. I am wild about animals – **EVERY** make and model. I guess Noah was the perfect name for me, you know, like Noah's Ark. My favorite critters are little pink pigs and dinosaurs. I like pigs because they're so cute and squealy, and I like dinosaurs because they are **BIG** and **STRONG**. I know they're nothing alike, but I think they are the neatest creatures God ever created.

Everything God creates is special in its very own different way. I love to read animal books... my Nana gives me **LOTS** of those! God made dinosaurs strong enough to lift a whole tree, but pigs aren't very strong at all. They need someone to take care of them. I'm very small too, and I can't do all the things that bigger kids can do, but God made me just the way I am for a special reason.

I have really bad food allergies, and that's one of the things that makes me smaller than other children. Being allergic to a lot of foods can be really tough sometimes. But I get lots of yummy homemade things, like mommy-made cookies, and biscuits. My tummy is just fine with that!

One time Daddy told me something cool. "Noah, God made you just the way you are, in a special, unique way. If He made you taller, you wouldn't be as close to the pretty flowers you always pick for Mommy." I thought about that a little bit. Whenever I pick her flowers, it always gives her a big smile! I guess God knew what He was doing there. Then Daddy swooped me up over his head. "And because you're not very heavy, I can lift you high up in the air and carry you on my shoulders! God doesn't make any mistakes."

Daddy knew what he was talking about. The way God makes us is for a special reason, just like He made the animals. If the piggies were as strong as dinosaurs, they wouldn't be so cute. Then I wouldn't giggle every time I look at them. If dinosaurs were small like piggies, they wouldn't be able to take care of the little guys. God knows what He's doing– always! So I'll trust Him. I'm one of His one of a kind creations, and so are you. He made us to do special things that only we can do. And He thinks we're **JUST RIGHT**!

Today's Talk to Jesus

Dear Jesus,

Thank You for taking care of me every day of my life. Help me to always remember that You made me just right, just the way I am. And help all the other kids like me to know that You made them just right too. Help me be **ALL** You want me to be. I know I'm little, but you love me in the **BIGGEST** way!

In Your precious name, Jesus. ~ Love, Me

My Bestest Friend Forever

No one shows greater love than when he lays down his life for his friends. – John 15:13 ISV

My name is Ladybug. Well, that's what my daddy and big brother call me. I'm excited to tell you all about my BFF! Do you know what BFF means? It's kind of a secret code for "Best Friend Forever"! Do you know who my best friend is? It's no secret! If I could climb up to the tip top of the tallest tree, I would shout it out to the whole entire world because I'm so proud of Him! Jesus is my BFF! There is no other Friend at all like Him. He is so sweet, and He loves children like you and me, with all of His heart! And He has a Big, **BIG** heart… so that's a whole lot of love!

Do you want to know another important secret? Come a little closer and I'll tell you. Shhhhh… Give me your ear… Jesus wants to be **YOUR** BFF too! He loves you more than you could ever imagine! He gave everything He had so that you could be His friend. The Bible says that no one can show any greater love than to give up his life for his friends. That's what Jesus did for us. When He was on the cross, He was thinking about you and me. He wanted to make a way for us to be with Him forever, in a perfect home that He's building just for us.

I heard my pastor say it this way: "I asked Jesus, 'How much do you love me?' And Jesus said, 'This much.' Then He stretched out His arms on the cross and He died for me." That's more love than we could ever even try to imagine and it comes straight from His Father's heart. Jesus loves us with love that is **WAY** more than perfect. No matter what we do, He loves us. No matter what we say, He loves us. We can tell Him absolutely anything. If we don't feel good, He wants us to talk to Him about it, even though He already knows how we feel. When we cry, He cries too. When we're sad, He's right beside us, wiping our tears away. When we hurt, He understands. His heart even hurts with us. He will **ALWAYS** be here for us because He knows exactly how it feels to hurt. And when we smile, He smiles even **BIGGER**.

I've been thinking how I want to be a really good BFF for Jesus because He's a perfect best friend to me. I want to make Him smile and show Him how much I love Him too. We can reach out our arms and send Him a **GIGANTIC** hug! I'm giving Him one right now! And, whenever we show His love to other people, it makes *Him* smile too. Let's go find someone who's hurting and let them know about our BFF. Let's tell everyone all about how Jesus loves them with all of His heart, and He wants to be their best friend too.

Today's Talk to Jesus

Dear Jesus,

Thank You for loving me with Your **AMAIZING** love. You'll always be the very best friend I will ever have. I know there are a whole lot of people who need Your love a whole lot. Help me to tell them all about You, so they can have You for their perfect best friend too. I sure do love You.

In Your precious name, Jesus. ~ Love, Me

Helping Hearts

Feed the hungry! Help those in trouble! Then your light will shine out from the darkness, and the darkness around you shall be as bright as day. – Isaiah 58:10 TLB

Hey there! Come on, I wanna show you something. This is my little puppy, Buttercup. She loves to lick my ice-cream cones. **YUM!** You want some too? I bet you're wondering what I'm called. Well, Mommy calls me Peanut. If you want to, you can call me that too. Mommy said when I was born I was itty-bitty, just like a peanut. So that's how I got my nickname. I'm still really little, but I've had some really big problems lately. My Doc says I have cancer. And we have to make tons of trips to the hospital. Sometimes I have to take special medicine that makes my tummy hurt. Mommy gets sad when I don't feel good. She always holds me and gives me the best hugs **EVER!** Just being with her makes me feel a whole lot better.

I have lots of people taking care of me. I have two doctors, and a whole bunch of nurses. And they're all trying really hard to help me get better. Mommy and Daddy do their best to take extra great care of me. My Grandpa and Grammy come see me a lot, they're my buddies. My silly friends make me smile and giggle. And I know I have a lot of people helping me, but sometimes when I'm alone, I cry. I'm tired of being sick and I wish this awful stuff would just go away. Whenever I feel like that, I remember my best Friend– Jesus. He's always here to cheer me up, and help me, and hold me.

One day I wheeled myself down the hospital hallway in my wheelchair. I like spying, so I peeked in all the rooms. There were lots of other sick children, just like me. I started thinking about things I could do to help those children. I could make them smile by being a friend and talking to them. I know how they feel because I know what it's like to be sick. I can share a balloon or draw them a picture. So many people help me all the time. I want to give someone a smile too. When I do that, I'm being a shining light for Jesus! When I bring a smile to another child, it makes my smile even bigger.

Today's Talk to Jesus

Dear Jesus,

Thank You for all the people who help me. Please let them know I'm so thankful for what they do to take care of me. Thank You for showing me how I can help other children who might be lonely or sad, like I am sometimes. I want to tell them how much You love me and how much You love them too. I just love being a bright little shining light for You!

In Your precious name, Jesus. ~ Love, Me

devotion 24

My Brother Jesus

Whoever does the will of my father in heaven is my brother, and sister, and mother." – Matthew 12:50 NIV

The fish sure are biting good today! I'm so glad you could come fishin' with me. I love to reel in the big ones. Look at the size of **HIM**! My name is Micah. I'm Jesus' brother… and so are you! Well, unless you're a girl, then you're his sister. Whoa… I bet you've got your eyes wide open now! Don't worry. I'll explain it all to you.

Jesus loves us so much that He gave His life for us. He wants us to love Him back and do what His Father wants us to do. In the Bible, He said it this way, "Anyone that loves My Father and does what He wants them to, they are My brothers and sisters."

See. I told you. Isn't it awesome? If you love Jesus and obey His Word, you become His brother or sister. How does it feel to have royal blood flowing through you? I really like having the King of kings as my big Brother! How about you? We have all kinds of fun together. He's the **BEST**, and He's always with me.

There's nothing like a big Brother to help get us through tough times. He's always here to help us, whatever we're doing, Especially while we're fishing! I think **THAT'S** His favorite. And He goes through everything with us… every hurt, every bad day, and every time we cry. He's always protecting us. And when we're afraid, He's right there to chase away our fears. He's the best big Brother we could ever, **EVER** have.

He understands us because He lived here on the earth too, just like us. He knew what it was like to be afraid. His tummy even growled when He was hungry, especially if He didn't catch any fish when He went fishing. He knows exactly what it's like. He understands everything we go through. He chose to come down here to earth and live like we do, bad days and all, so that one day we can go up to Heaven and live with Him forever. I bet He just can't wait to take us fishing! And I sure can't wait to catch a whole bunch of big ones with Him. I love my big Brother, and I'm so glad I'm His little brother!

Today's Talk to Jesus

Dear Jesus,

Thank You for leaving Heaven and coming to live on earth. I know it must have been so hard for You, when You were here and people were mean to you. I know You must have been so afraid, but You still went through everything just for us. You even died for us so we could be with you forever, in Heaven. I want to be just like You. I'm so glad I have You for my big Brother. I'll follow in Your footsteps. Help me to remember that You know exactly everything I'm going through and you're going through it with me. I want to be the best little brother for You I could ever be.

In Your precious name, Jesus. ~ Love, Me

My Heavenly Daddy

You received God's Spirit when he adopted you as His own children. Now we call him, "Abba, Father." – Romans 8:15 NLT

I'm Lissa and I love my Daddy with all my heart. I don't have very many things of my own, but I have **SO** much joy in my heart. I have to share my toys and dresses with my sister. Some of my dresses have holes, and my toys are getting old. But I'm the richest little girl ever because I have the sweetest Daddy in the whole big wide world. Sometimes people don't know exactly what I mean when I say that because I've never even met my dad here. But I do know God, my Heavenly Daddy. And He loves me with love that's so big and beautiful I could never even understand it. His love fills up my heart and **OVERWHELMS** me. The Bible says that nothing– and that means **NOTHING**– can ever separate us from **HIS LOVE**.

My dad on earth left our family when I was a little baby. I don't really understand why, but I know one thing… My Heavenly Daddy will never ever leave me by myself. He always knows how I feel and He understands when I hurt. He knows all my pain, and He cries when I cry. I have a rare kind of cancer, and I can't walk. But in my heart, my Daddy carries me wherever I go. Sometimes we have a lot of hospital bills to pay, but my Daddy always gives us everything we need in **AMAZING** ways that really surprise us. He's so perfect! I sure can't wait for my sweet Daddy to pick me up and spin me around and around one day!

My mommy read a verse to me the other day. It says that God has adopted us, so we're His own children! And now we can call Him, **Abba** Father– that word means **DADDY**! He is our sweet, perfect Daddy. And He holds us tight in His arms. He cherishes us just as if each one of us is His **ONLY** child. The verse also says He gave us His Spirit. That means He is always with us and He lives inside us. We are never all by ourselves, and we never will be. And the very best thing is that He is Daddy to all of us, even my mommy, and my grammy and my papaw. He's Daddy to you too! And He will be… forever!

Today's Talk to Jesus

Dear Jesus,

Thank You so much for adopting me into Your family. You loved us so much that You hurt for us on the cross so we could be with You forever! Thank you, Jesus, for sharing your sweet Daddy with me, and making a way so God can be my Daddy too. I want the whole world to know that I love You, and that I'm so glad to be my Daddy's little girl.

In Your precious name, Jesus. ~ Love, Me

Creator of the Universe

I stand in awe of your deeds, LORD. – Habakkuk 3:2 NIV

Hi there! My name is Owen. I'm five years old! And I just had an incredible birthday party, right here in my hospital room! You see, I have leukemia and I'm living here at the hospital for a while. My parents gave me a really cool telescope for my birthday. Have you ever seen a telescope? Let me show you how my telescope works. It makes things that are far away look really close. It's a stellar experience! My favorite thing to do with my telescope is to zoom in on those amazing stars that God put up there! I love to study the stars and planets. Outer space is **SO** super awesome!

Do you know what's even more amazing? Our mighty God created all of the billions and zillions of stars! He made the moon and **ALL** the planets like Mars, Jupiter, and Pluto. Then there are the comets that **ZOOM** across the sky and all the galaxies that make up the entire universe! Isn't it just **MEGA** ginormously cool? God is so powerful! He created all of that by just talking. He spoke, and the stars glowed in the night sky– just like that! He is **ALL** powerful!

Every time I look at the stars, I remember just how powerful and mighty God is and how He cares about us **SO** much. He loved us so much that He sent His one and only Son to die for us so that we could live with Him in Heaven forever. It was all part of His plan. Just think... it must have been so hard for Him to create the hill that Jesus died on. He had to actually grow the tree that would one day be made into a cross for His only Son. It's so hard for me to think about it, but that's what pure love must be. It had to hurt His heart more than we could ever know, but He did it just because He loves us.

God made our earth just perfect for us to live in because His love for us is so **BIG** and amazing. He made things just right so it doesn't get too hot or too cold, like on Neptune and Mercury. And I'm so thankful we don't get those terrible storms like Uranus does. There's not one planet that compares to our beautiful earth. It has water, trees, plants, and animals. Everything we could ever need or want, God gave us. Now you know why I love looking through my telescope. It reminds me that the God who **HOLDS** the universe in His hands, is holding me on His lap.

Today's Talk to Jesus

Dear Jesus,

Thank You for making all the amazing stars and planets with Your Father. Everything you are and everything you do is perfect. I want the things I do to be perfect for You. I want to show You how much I love You because You show me every day how much You love me. Thank You for dying on the cross for me because You love me. There are so many things about You that amaze me, but nothing can compare with Your **PERFECT** love. It's **WAY** bigger than the entire universe!

In Your precious name, Jesus. ~ Love, Me

A Heavenly Home

He will wipe every tear from their eyes, and there will be no more death or sorrow or crying or pain. All these things are gone forever. – Revelation 21:4 NLT

Hi there! My name is Sandy, and this is my ducky– Chucky. I just can't wait to tell you all about the greatest, coolest, most amazingly awesome place ever! Part of my family already lives there. Even though I miss them whole bunches, I'm so happy when I think about what it's like for them right now! It's a place where everyone smiles and laughs a lot! All the kids are playing their favorite games there, and they can always be happy. Not one person ever makes fun of them or says mean things to anyone. I know it's hard to believe, or even imagine, but it's true. Nobody hurts anyone's feelings there. There are never any people who do bad things there. And everything is perfect, just like things were always meant to be.

It's a **REAL** place that's bright and cheerful with all of God's most perfect blessings. We never have to be sad there because God will wipe away all our tears. I know that all those wonderful blessings are hard to even understand… but wait, there are even more blessings in this perfect place. No one is ever, ever sick there. Pain isn't something you even have to know about, and we **NEVER** have to say goodbye to anyone we love. Can you imagine that? And it's a wonderful place filled with all our favorite things. Do you want to know the name of this special place so you can tell your Daddy to put it in his GPS and take you there? This perfect place is Heaven! It's also called Paradise. Your daddy's GPS can't tell you how to get there, but God has His own GPS that tells us how to get to Heaven. His GPS is God's Plan of Salvation. It's the Bible. It helps lost people find their way to Heaven.

The Bible is our treasure map to Heaven! It tells us all about how God sent His only Son, Jesus, to die for us. Then Jesus rose again to Heaven, so He could make everything ready for when we get there! And if we ask Him to come into our hearts and forgive us of our sins, He will. If we believe in Him, and He lives in our heart, then we will be with Him in Heaven someday. And we'll be with Him forever and ever! On the great treasure map, Heaven marks the spot! I'll see you there!

Today's Talk to Jesus

Dear Jesus,

Thank You for leaving Your super special home in Heaven and coming to die for me so I can live with You in the greatest place ever, forever! I can't wait! You'll be in my heart forever, and I'll be in your heart too! I love You bunches!

In Your precious name, Jesus. ~ Love, Me

Baaaaaaa!

He gathers the lambs in his arms, and carries them close to his heart. – Isaiah 40:11 NIV

Hi! I'm Timmy, and I've got a very important message from Jesus, for **YOU**! Are you ready? Jesus wants you to know… He loves you soooo much, and He wants to carry you in His arms! Do you know why? Because you'll be way closer to His heart if you're in His arms. Jesus wants to keep you close to His heart, and spend time with you **FOREVER**. He wants to always be with you, wherever you go!

One day I went fishing with my gramps, and we caught a whole bunch of **BIG**, yummy ones. On the way home, we saw a **HUGE** red barn with a real rooster on top! And there were lots of fluffy sheep all around the barn. Gramps stopped to rest under a tree, and looked down at me. He rubbed my hair and messed it all up. He said, "Timmy, did you know God has a farm?" I just couldn't believe my ears, "That's just silly, Gramps!" But, he said "No, it's not." Then he sat on the ground beside me, and opened up His Bible. "Here, if you don't believe me, I'll prove it to you from God's Word… See, Timmy, it says it right here… we are His sheep and Jesus is our Shepherd. He takes care of us and guards us **EVERY** minute of **EVERY** day. When we don't feel good, He holds us right up close to His heart."

Sometimes, when it's just Jesus and me, I can almost hear His heart beating. He loves to hold us that close to His precious heart. And when we hurt and can't walk by ourselves, Jesus carries us! When Mommy takes me places, I see other kids running all around everywhere. I get kind of sad because I can't do that… I have to ride in my wheelchair. But then I remember what Gramps told me next. "Timmy, Jesus loves you so much… He gives you a piggyback ride!" And, that brought all my giggles out! It's just **SO** awesome being His little lamb. It's not baaaaaaad at all! I'm **SO** glad to be riding in my Shepherd's arms.

Today's Talk to Jesus

Dear Jesus,

Thank You for carrying me! Your big, strong arms keep me safe and loved. When I can't do all the things other kids can, help me to remember all the awesome things I **CAN** do! I know that I'm always in Your arms, and that You love me **JUST** the way I am. I know You're holding me right now. Here's a super **HUGE** hug for you! I'm really glad You're my Shepherd— I just love being Your little lamb!

In Your precious name, Jesus. ~ Love, Me

Angels Around Me

"See that you do not despise one of these little ones. For I tell you that their angels in heaven always see the face of my Father in heaven." – Matthew 18:10 NIV

I'm so glad you're finally here. I've been waiting for you to get here all day! Oh, let me tell you who I am. My name is Lucy and my most favorite thing in the **WHOLE** wide world is my little fluffy-puffy white kitten, Angel. Mommy and Daddy gave her to me when they first told me I had a rare kind of cancer. They said she would help me to remember that God has given me my very own personal guardian angels to take care of me. Jesus said in the Bible that God loves me so much He sends His special angels to take care of me– I even have angels watching me **RIGHT NOW**!

I always get a little nervous the night before I have to go to the hospital and have my treatments. I get my little kitty and put her on my lap. Then sometimes I start singing songs to Jesus. That makes my fears go away almost every time. I even make up songs for Jesus. Last week I made up this song: *Be on the lookout for angels 'cause God's got them on the lookout for you.* I know it might sound silly, but my little song made me stronger and helped a lot. I really think Jesus gave me my special little song to help me, just like He gave songs to David in the Bible when he was a little boy taking care his father's sheep. He had **MIGHTY** angels taking care of Him too, while he protected the sheep against **HUGE**, ferocious animals.

Wow! It's just so amazing when I think about how God loves us **SO** much that He sends His special angels to take care of us. Heavenly angels, who spend time in Heaven with God, are watching **US**... little you and me. I wonder what my angel's name is??? I bet I'll get to meet him one day. I'll give my angel and God a **GIANT** hug! God is like our Daddy in Heaven who sends His special friends to protect us. Just think about that. The same angels who take care of *us,* actually spend time with the Creator of the universe! Now that should help us not to be afraid and to trust God no matter what we're going through. And just think, one day we'll get to live with our Heavenly Daddy too. He will hold us on His lap, and squeeze us even tighter than I squeeze my fluffy kitty, Angel. And I just can't wait to see the sweet smile on His face, just like the angels get to see.

Today's Talk to Jesus

Dear Jesus,

Thank You for always sending Your big, strong angels to guard me and keep me safe. Your love is **AMAZING**! It's way bigger than Your **WHOLE** creation! I love You all the way to the moon and back.

In Your precious name, Jesus. ~ Love, Me

Look! There's Jesus!

"No one knows when that day or hour will come. Even the angels in Heaven and the Son don't know. Only the Father knows."
— Matthew 24:36 GW

Hey there! I'm Zach. I love to go on long trips in our car. My very favorite place to go is Grammy's house! I think my Grammy deserves the **GRAMMY AWARD** for all of the **SUPER COOL** stuff she does with me. We go to the zoo, and the big park, and the beach. It's **SO** much fun! Well, it was before I got cancer. Now I can't really take vacations because I always have to go to the doctor or the hospital. I can't go too far away for very long.

One time when I had to stay home, I was really sad. My friend was having a **HUGE** birthday party. It was going to have a bounce house, a water slide, ice-cream cones, and even cotton candy! But I couldn't go because I had to stay in the hospital. Grammy said, "Don't worry, Zach. If we can't go to the party, I'll bring the party to **YOU!**" She really did it too. She brought in a **BIG** bunch of bright balloons and party bags with goodies and toys to share with the other kids who were sick. She made everything perfect! Now do you know why I think my Grammy needs to win a Grammy Award?

My mom and dad are counting the days 'till we can go on a long vacation again. They said once I finish my treatments, we will celebrate and go on another awesome trip. I think we're going to the beach! It's hard to be patient and wait for my treatments to be all done, but it's not much longer now.

When we finally get in the car, buckle up our seatbelts, and head for our favorite beach, I always ask over and over, "Are we there yet?" I'm not a very patient patient, even when I'm not at the doctor's office. Sometimes it helps make the time go by faster when I think about where I'm going, and make a list of all the fun things I want to do when we get there. Before I know it, we're already there!

That makes me think of the forever vacation we'll take in Heaven when Jesus comes to take us home. I like to think about how incredible it will be when we get there. I'm excited because I won't ever have to go to the doctor again. Mom, Dad, and Grammy will be there too. It will be the most awesome family reunion ever. One day Jesus will take us all home, to our really real home. I better go look out the window because any minute He could be here! Pretty soon we'll be saying, "Look! There's Jesus!"

Today's Talk to Jesus

Dear Jesus,

I'm so excited that I'm **REALLY** going to live with You forever and ever. I know it will be the most fun time we'll ever have! I can't wait to see You coming to get us. I'm going to give You the biggest and best hug you've ever had! Help us remember to think about our "forever vacation" to Heaven, our perfect home! I'll always be looking and watching for You. And I know you're always watching me too.

In Your precious name, Jesus. ~ Love, Me

Letter from Jesus

The Father . . . loved us so much, that we are called children of God. And we really are His children. – 1 John 3:1 ICB

My name is Jesus. I am the Alpha and Omega, the Beginning and the End. I want to share something special with you, right from my heart. I want you to know just how much your Heavenly Daddy loves you. His love for you is more than **All** the sand on all of the beaches! His love for you is more than **All** the stars in the whole universe! No matter what you do, He loves you. No matter what you say, He loves you. **NOTHING** can ever take His love away from you... If I tried to tell you from now until forever, I could never explain how **BIG** and **PERFECT** His love is for you.

You are more precious to Him than anything. He loves you as if you are the **ONLY** child He has. His love for you is so amazing that He sent Me– His Son, Jesus– to give my life for you, so that you can be with Him forever! I came to the earth to show you that your Heavenly Daddy loves you more than you could ever begin to understand. I left everything I had in Heaven, and My Father, to come and die for you... so that you could know how much He loves you. You are so perfect and precious to Him that He made a way for you to live with Him, and Me, forever. All you have to do is believe that I died for you, to forgive you. Love me with all your heart, and live for me. You are your Daddy's precious, priceless treasure.

Can I ask you a special question? Have you ever invited Me into your heart? I can come and live inside you if you invite me in. I want to live in your precious heart. I want to be part of everything in your life, and be your very best Friend forever! There is a special prayer at the end of this page. If you pray this prayer from your heart, you will be with Me and our Daddy, in our perfect home forever one day. Right now I'm busy building a special home for you and filling it with all your favorite things. I'll be coming soon, to bring all of Daddy's children home. I just know you'll love it. I can't wait to spend forever loving you.

Love, Me!

The Most Important Talk to Jesus Ever

Dear Jesus,

I know You love me more than I could ever imagine! I believe You died on the cross for me so that I can live with You forever in Heaven. I'm so sorry for the things I've done that made You sad. Please forgive me. I want You to come and live inside my heart. I want to live for You and love You with my whole heart. I can't wait to see the beautiful new home You've made for me! I know it's going to be just perfect. You are everything to me, and I'll love You forever.

In Your precious name, Jesus. ~ Love, Me

Thank you...

I'd like to thank some very special people for helping and encouraging me during this eight-year journey of writing My Walk With Jesus Devotional Bible.

To my family— My dad, my mom, and my sweet little brother. Thank you for always being here for me. I could never have written this book without all of the love, support, and help you have given me. I love you!

To my grandparents, "Nana" and "Papaw"— Thank you for inspiring my love for books since I was a little tiny girl. Thank you for always encouraging me to write for Jesus! I love you!

To my editor, Dixie Phillips— Thank you for sharing your amazing talent as you helped to bring this book to life, and encourage precious children.

To Bruce Marchiano— Thank you for your incredibly special portrayal of Jesus that shows His perfect love. Through it you've inspired much of what I have written in this book. Thank you for helping me to use these photos of Jesus to show His love to many precious children.

To Sharon Puterbaugh— Thank you for helping me find the photos of Bruce portraying Jesus for my book!

To Chris Tomlin— Thank you for your incredible music about Jesus. You have inspired MWWJDB in an amazing way, as I have listened to your songs countless times while writing this book!

To God, my Daddy in Heaven, and to Jesus— Thank You for Your perfect love. Thank You for giving me the words You wanted me to share with Your precious children. Please let this book help many to understand Your perfect love for all of us. I love You with all my heart!

Check out My Walk With Jesus Devotional Bible Online!

Website— MWWJDB.com

Facebook—

facebook.com/OfficalMyWalkWithJesusBible

Twitter— @MWWJDB

Follow Jenna Sue Bennett Online!

Facebook— facebook.com/officialJenna

Twitter— @JennaSue_Author

About the Author...

Jenna Sue Bennett is blessed with a desire in her heart to write. At the age of ten, she began writing My Walk With Jesus Devotional Bible, completing it before her eighteenth birthday. She will be using the profits from this book to share it with children around the world. It is a dream come true for her to use her writing gift to share Jesus' love with children facing cancer, and their families.

In her free time, Jenna enjoys spending time with her loving parents, and her sweet and silly little brother. Boating, camping, fishing, and taking long sunset walks are some of her favorite ways to spend time with her family.

Jenna has also published another children's book titled "My Little Dog, Fifi". It was written when she was seven, and is available for purchase online.

Jenna hopes to write many more books that will show children how the love of Jesus is with them always. She is also writing a fictional novel based on the lives of Jesus' disciples. She prays that all of her writing projects will bring many people closer to God!

www.ingramcontent.com/pod-product-compliance
Lightning Source LLC
Chambersburg PA
CBHW060811090426
42737CB00002B/30